DIVIDE NINE

Cliff Green

Dedication

To Dee,
I'm not sure why God made me wait so long to find you.
I guess He was testing my patience.

The tREAL 11111111111111111111111111111111

Passion & Purpose

Wilkinsburg

Being **A tREAL O.G.**

Preface

The title Divide 9 was divinely inspired by the Most High. My studies have shown that Black people are 9 ether beings. If you examine a strand of our hair, you'll notice it curls into a 9. Our hair acts as an antenna that receives downloads from the ether around us.

There are forces intentionally withholding knowledge from humanity. There was a time when ether or aether was taught to people. Ether is the forgotten element that permeates everything around us. They don't want us to reconnect with ether.

The title 'Divide 9' is a play on words with 'Divine 9', which refers to the Black Greek Letter Organizations (BGLOs). These groups include five fraternities and four sororities. In my opinion, the BGLOs have contributed more to our division than to our unity.

Even though I briefly discuss BGLOs, this book isn't about them, and my goal isn't to criticize my brothers and sisters who are members. I want to enlighten some, but I might offend others. You can't please everyone, even if what you say is true. People will always find a way to be offended.

I want to inspire you to live by the truth, no matter who you might offend. I want to give you the courage to be your most genuine self. I hope you never hesitate to express yourself and showcase your gifts, talents, and abilities.

People will try to dim your light, including those you know and love. You have the right to use all your gifts, even if others don't understand you.

Look at this book's cover. Do you think everyone will understand all its meanings? Probably not. But I won't let that stop me from sharing these gems.

9 represents completion. The year 2025, when you add its digits, totals 9 (2 + 0 + 2 + 5 = 9). Below the 9 on the cover, you see my first name, CLIFF, but what about my last name? Do you see it? What color is the book?

Let me clarify some of the less obvious details on the cover. Have you heard of the 369 Hz frequency that is often associated with the scientist Nikola Tesla? Tesla worked with electricity and high-energy concepts.

What do you see on the back cover? You see a '3' designed like a lightning bolt. This is the third book, completing the **A tREAL O.G.** series. Lightning is the highest form of electricity, and with this book, I plan to shock the world! A '9' when flipped is a '6'. The cover has a hidden 369 Hz frequency.

When you open the book and lay it flat with the cover side up, you'll notice both the '3' and the '9'. I have been on Earth for 39 years. This book was published on November 16, 2025, which is 11/16/2025 or 111 (3), 6, 9. The 3 also represents the 300 pages in the **A tREAL O.G.** series.

Someday, your light will shine so brightly that it can't be ignored. I pray this book inspires you to never dim your light.

It is an honor to present to you Divide 9.

Table of Contents

November, I'm Back!

I hope this message enlightens you. We're living by the wrong calendar. There are things we've been told that aren't true. For example, November is actually the ninth month. November comes from the Latin word novem, meaning nine.

November is a special month for me because my birthday is on the 30th! I published 'Less Than a Sack of Weed' in November 2020, and I released this book in November 2025.

I've always wondered if I am the reincarnation of my grandpa, William. He passed away in February of '85, nine months before I was born. I've been told that I have an old soul. Plus, I don't fit in with today's society.

Knowing this is a year of completion, I wonder if it will be my last time reincarnated. Will I get it right this time? Will I finish the mission the Most High has assigned to me? And before anyone gets scared, I believe I still have 60 or more years left here on Earth. I don't plan on leaving anytime soon.

I can't confirm or deny reincarnation, but I have some theories. One is that if you get it right, you become a star shining brightly in the night sky. The other is that if you get it wrong, you come back as a human or an animal, depending on how you lived your life.

These are just theories. Don't let them overwhelm you. This book was written to help you develop your own ideas and theories.

Scare Tactics

There is always propaganda designed to instill fear in your heart. Let's go back a few years and look at the word Ebola. I'll share my etymological breakdown. Etymology is the study of the origin of words to reveal their true or hidden meanings.

Ebola, when you say it out loud, sounds like 'e-bowl-lie' because that's what it really was: an extra bowl of lies. The lies about Ebola were created to distract us. Ebola may have been real, but most of us will never know because we've only seen it on TV.

Our minds are constantly fed lies, deception, and fear. The people controlling the media are attacking our minds because they know that scared people are easier to control. I know you've noticed how everything on TV seems dark and negative. Their goal is to keep us in a constant state of fear.

When they recognize that fear is deeply ingrained in our hearts, minds, and souls, they offer a solution. Unbeknownst to us, their solution takes away our freedom. They know that if you feel safe, you won't mind losing your freedom. Because, hey, it's for the greater good.

Look at what happened after 9/11. After all the propaganda about upcoming terrorist attacks, what happened? TSA agents are conducting pat-down searches at the airport. Our phone calls and texts are recorded. Cameras are everywhere. They're not looking for terrorists; they're watching every move we make.

The military has acquired more weapons, and they are patrolling American streets. They were testing the waters with the military presence in Ferguson a few years ago.

They presented the laws and acts to us claiming safety and patriotism. What they truly wanted was to see how much people could take before pushing back.

Ask yourself, what happened to Anthrax, West Nile, H1N1, Swine flu, Mad Cow disease, C-19, and so on? When they realized the fear wasn't high enough, they went back to the drawing board and started working on their next project.

The news constantly bombards us with issues meant to distract us from focusing and reconnecting with our divine selves. I realized their programming worked when this lady told me she wouldn't interact with people from Africa because of Ebola.

They never show us how beautiful Africa truly is. Africa is rich in natural resources. Most of the technology we use wouldn't work without minerals from Africa.

Why does the media always portray Africa negatively? They claimed AIDS originated in Africa, but that was a lie. They said Ebola started there, but that was a lie. After researching, you'll find that many diseases were actually engineered to wipe out Africans.

Even though I don't believe the slave narrative as it has been told to us, for this story's purpose, let's go with what we've been told. America and capitalism itself wouldn't be what they are today without the most significant resource to date, which was free African labor.

The system's goal has always been to prevent people from discovering the truth. They use viruses, germs, and diseases to attack our minds.

Do you remember the terrorist group Isis? It's funny that they chose the name Isis. Isis is the Greek name for an ancient Egyptian goddess. Her Egyptian name is Auset. Her husband's name is Ausar or Osiris.

They chose the name Isis because they know the Willie Lynch chip is being removed. That's why they try to scare us away from everything that embodies our true selves. We are gods and goddesses!

They divided nine ether beings because we are becoming the gods and goddesses that the Most High intended us to be. Our women are embracing their God-given hair. They are mirroring the image of Isis.

This system depends on our self-hatred. The controllers know that people who love themselves can't be controlled, nor will they support a system trying to prevent them from reaching their divinity.

I relate many things to being Black because of my experience as a Black man, but this is my call to everyone to break free from the lies they keep perpetuating. Only then will people be able to come together and heal. They will not be able to divide or conquer us!

Magnesium Oil

We should be cautious when selecting lotions and soaps. A lot of products contain harmful chemicals that can damage our health. Remember what I said about toothpaste in "Do You Swallow?"[1]. The fluoride in toothpaste is considered poisonous when swallowed.

I try my best to use all-natural products, and I think you should too. A natural product that I love is magnesium oil. It offers so many benefits, including enhanced sleep, improved skin, stress relief, relief from joint and muscle pain, and it gives you an energy boost.

Magnesium oil is a game-changer. I use it daily and can vouch for its effectiveness. It's so good that I bought a bottle for each member of my family.

A lot of people are magnesium-deficient. Eating a bag of spinach every day still wouldn't be enough. Using magnesium oil can help make up for the deficiency.

The most effective way to gain the benefits of it is through your skin. This method is called transdermal absorption. Our pores are open after we shower, making it the best time to apply magnesium oil so it can be absorbed into our system.

Give magnesium oil a try, and you'll wish you'd tried it sooner.

---

[1] Green, Cliff. "Do You Swallow?". *Order Over Chaos*, 2024, pp 64 - 65

The Way of the Wise

The book of Proverbs is a collection of wisdom. Proverbs 31 was a powerful way to end the book. Verses one through nine describe the qualities of a king, while verses ten through thirty-one focus on the qualities of a noble queen.

Anyone seeking to become a leader should study and apply the lessons found in Proverbs. The book is filled with gems. You could read and re-read it a thousand times and learn something every time.

A key lesson from Proverbs 31 is to stay clear-headed. Kings shouldn't indulge in the same things as everyone else, like alcohol and drugs. I'm not saying I never drank, but as I focus on my purpose, alcohol no longer benefits me. Actually, it never did, but I'm human and fell for it. I hope this reaches you before you do.

Being clear-headed and vigilant is a king's duty. Have you ever tried to work out after a night of drinking? It's hard to do. I can't write books with chapters called "Temple,"[2] and be destroying mine.

Are there books or chapters in the Bible that you enjoy? Do you read the Bible? Is it the true and living Word of God? Or is it a tool for controlling and enslaving people? Is it plagiarized from other ancient texts?

When you have a chance, take a look at Proverbs 31 and answer the questions above. Don't worry, this isn't a Bible-thumping book - it's just a book written by a man, like all the others.

---

[2] Green, Cliff. "Temple". *Order Over Chaos*, 2024, p 69

I read the Bible and have prospered greatly from doing so. We need to be wise enough to extract valuable lessons from everything we read and experience. You may not agree with everything I say, but you should take the jewels and apply them to your life.

You might know, but if you're not applying what you know, you're not being wise. The way of the wise is to use the knowledge you've obtained through your experiences to better yourself and others.

Decisions

Some people never learn. They consistently make poor decisions, receive only light reprimands, and then repeat the same mistakes. They might face worse consequences the second time, but it's still a slap on the wrist.

Somehow, it never seems to sink in that their actions have consequences. Maybe that's the thrill of it. Maybe they think they won't get caught this time. It hasn't worked before, but maybe it will this time. The third time's the charm, right?

They do the same thing only to end up with the short end of the stick. And boom! They get caught, and they face the harshest judgment of their lives.

God says, "Look! I'm going to sit you down for a while so you can reflect on your decisions and how they've brought you to where you are. I know things seem grim, but if you show me sincerity, obedience, and faith, I will guide you to a better place. Got it?"

Of course, they respond with a promise to do the right thing! Some people only listen to God when they're in the worst situations. Their promises sound good when they're at the end of their rope. Sometimes, that's what it takes for the message to be heard.

After sitting for so long, God finally allows them to stand up. They start walking a little and realize they never forgot how to walk in the first place.

They take a few steps and immediately forget their promise to God, turning away from the path they vowed to follow. God sends them one last sign to remind them of that promise. This sign might come as a person, a life-changing event, or just a voice in their head.

God says, "I've given you every opportunity in the world to get it right. This will be the last bone I throw you. Make the right decision!"

Everyone has promised God to do better, only to fall short. But we should take our promises to God seriously, because some people don't get a second chance, let alone a third.

If you're lucky enough to get one, try to make the best choices to avoid repeating your past mistakes. Otherwise, you might end up sitting down again.

You should think before you act. That's how you make wise decisions.

The Chicken or the Egg

The idea that wisdom comes with age isn't always true. This has become evident for many adults. Sometimes, older people appear more confused about life than the younger generation.

They enjoy discussing the behavior of youth, but they rarely take responsibility for their role in shaping how they act.

As I mentioned in "Family Equals Perfection,[3]" children imitate both good and bad behaviors of those around them when they lack parental figures. Plus, children are growing up with parents who are trying to be young.

When a parent chooses to be a friend instead of a parent, it often leads to a lack of respect in that relationship. Young people have lost respect for their elders. Honestly, I can't blame them. It's hard to respect people from whom you can't seek advice or encouragement.

For example, I was listening to two older people discussing relationships. It was a man and a woman, both around 50 years old. The woman said she suspected her husband might be unfaithful. Her reasoning had merit, but it wasn't enough to reach a definite conclusion.

---

[3] Green, Cliff. "Family Equals Perfection". *Less Than a Sack of Weed*, 2020, pp. 96 - 99

They talked about cheating and whether either of them had ever done it. She then explained that women are better at it.

Being as curious as I am, I asked her to explain why she thinks women are better cheaters. She laughed and said, "I'm not snitching on us! I'm not snitching on us!" I sat there, watching her and wondering why she thinks this is cute.

You're in your fifties, and I realize that people will do what they do. But when do they grow up? She never thought I was asking for relationship advice. Maybe I just wanted to know what to look for in a woman to avoid the headache.

I'm not saying we should constantly look for signs of cheating, but if they appear, it would be helpful to recognize them. She could have given me the game to make sure my Family Equals Perfection.[4] But her age didn't give her the wisdom to see that.

Hindsight is 20/20 because I should have pulled her aside and asked her some questions. But to return to my original point, why aren't elders teaching young people? It was the right time and place to give a young man some advice.

Young people lack the experience their elders have, which can keep them from knowing what questions to ask. Hopefully, someone will read this and

---

[4] Green, Cliff. "Family Equals Perfection". *Less Than a Sack of Weed*, 2020, pp. 96 - 99

recognize where they fell short. You can't complain about the youth, yet you've never shown them the way.[5]

To revisit the issue of young people not respecting their elders, should they be expected to? Yes, but it's difficult when they're not teaching us anything or setting a good example.

They're not pulling us aside and saying, "Son, look here...!" They don't do half of what they claim happened to them while growing up in the community. "Back when I was young, if you got in trouble, Mr. Johnson was going to get you; when you got home, your parents got you again." To today's youth, that sounds like nonsense.

If elders want to hold youth accountable for their behavior, they need to provide a model to follow. Because I can't tell which came first: the chicken or the egg.

[5] Green, Cliff. "Monkey See, Monkey Do". *Order Over Chaos*, 2024, pp. 70 - 71

N_gger

I was called a n_gger not too long ago. Yes, in 2025. I can't make this up.

The crazy part is that it didn't even bother me. How small-minded of him to think that a simple word could get a reaction out of me. Some might say I should have punched him. But if I had, I would have moved from a position of strength to one of weakness.

The state of weakness occurs when you make an emotional decision. I felt no particular way when he said it because I am superior to him mentally, physically, and spiritually. I operate from a position of power.

There is power in the knowledge of myself that I have. There is power in my God-given abilities. There is power in understanding who you truly are.

Stop being overly emotional all the time. Yes, anger is an emotion. It's hard to see clearly when all you see is red. I am speaking from experience because I am working to control my anger.

How would you feel or what would you do if someone called you names? Does every act of disrespect give you a reason to lose your temper? Has losing your temper been effective, or does it just make you feel better?

My boy calling me a nagger was justified. I was intentionally asking him questions about his relationship. I can't hold you, I wanted to swing on him when he said it, though!

Mentality

Living among my people is incredibly difficult. There's no safety in my community. I stayed to be a source of light and hope, but lately, I feel it's time for me to leave.

I hate that it has to be this way, but unfortunately, it is. I shouldn't have to worry about carrying a weapon while walking around my community, but most of the trouble I've encountered has come from people who look like me. That's a sad but true statement.

I'm amazed at how the original man, with all his godliness and abilities, has turned into a devil in today's world. When people tell you that their squad is demons, you should believe them.

I am becoming the man God intended me to be. *Men* on the same path need to unite and build. We are entering a new world where the weak will perish.

Men who don't change their ways will be left behind. Across America, towns are being rebuilt. *Men* are playing a real-life version of the game Monopoly. These *men* aim to take over the entire board.

Too many young Black *men* are repping neighborhoods that others are gentrifying. It's time to get serious! The world is changing, and if you plan to spend your whole life in the streets, trust me, you will lose to *men* who aim to own them.

Have you heard of a master plan? Every major city has one that outlines what will happen over the next 10, 20, or even 30 years. Have you heard the saying,

"Those who fail to plan, plan to fail!" How will you catch up with people who plan?

What would happen if the government decided to cut all programs? What if every kind of government aid disappeared? Can you provide shelter, food, and protection for your family?

These are questions that *men* ask themselves. *Men* seek to own land, houses, and property. That's what it means to have a *men*tality!

Nothin' to Play With

What happened to toys? Do kids still have imaginations? I believe they do, but people are harming their children's imaginations, brains, and eyesight by giving them phones and tablets. I wrote this before, and I will say it again. Technology isn't a babysitter![6]

I just saw a man give an iPhone to a four-year-old. Why does a four-year-old need a cell phone? I'll wait... Does anyone research or monitor what their kids do anymore?

All tablets, phones, and computer screens emit artificial light. Any light that is not sunlight, moonlight, or firelight is regarded as artificial. Artificial light can be harmful to our eyes.

Have you ever spent so much time on your computer or phone that you ended up with a headache or your eyes started to hurt? That is because the artificial light emitted by these devices damages our eyes and brain.

Since these devices can harm adults' eyes, wouldn't it be wise to consider that they might cause even greater damage to a child's developing eyes?

I wasn't planning to bring this up, but the Most High put this thought in my mind. Most of our children are born in hospitals. What's wrong with that, you might wonder?

---

[6] Green, Cliff. "Technology Isn't A Babysitter". *Order Over Chaos*, 2024, pp. 33 - 35

Consider what I just mentioned about artificial light. Aren't hospitals filled with it? Don't you think it might shock newborns, who spent nine months in darkness, to see artificial light when they come out of their mother's womb? Their pure souls probably sense that something is wrong.

Plus, I don't want just any random doctor to be the first person to touch or imprint on my child. Please tell me what to do, and I'll take care of it. Thanks! That might be a reason why so many people are struggling to break the chains.

They have been imprinted on since birth. Plus, parents allow their children to watch anything and everything, reinforcing the imprint.

You might be reading this book on a device. If so, wear blue light-blocking glasses and turn on your device's eye comfort mode.

To improve your eyesight, consider learning how to sun gaze, practicing eye exercises, wearing pinhole glasses, and spending time in nature. Use your eyes as the Most High intended us to use them. Make sure you're getting the proper nutrition daily.

Your kids' eyes and imagination depend on you! Now that you have this knowledge, how will you use it?

Bald-headed

"You bald-headed little girl! You're so F'n bad! I should slap the s**t out of you!" That's what I heard a lady tell her daughter as I sat there and waited to check out at the grocery store.

"Eww, they're going to arrest you because you didn't pay for that sucker! They're going to put you in cuffs and take you to jail." That's what she told her daughter as they walked out of the grocery store. I know it sounds cruel, and it is, but some people truly don't know any better. They're only copying what their parents did.

No one may have taught them that children's minds are meant to be molded. Parents should be mindful of everything they say and do around their children. Take that baby girl, for example: if her mother keeps filling her head with harmful comments, just as she has been, her daughter will probably internalize and believe them to be true.

Parents need to be even more vigilant about the outside influences they expose their children to, such as music, TV, games, and more. There are too many subliminal messages being transmitted through the media, and allowing your child to participate in them without carefully reviewing the content first is risky. If you haven't already, go read "Don't Talk to Strangers!"[7]

---

[7] Green, Cliff. "Don't Talk to Strangers! – Robin Green". *Order Over Chaos*, 2024, pp. 1 - 3

I have seen someone close to me pretending to engage in inappropriate behavior. Keep in mind, he was only four years old. When I asked where he learned that, he told me it was from someone on YouTube.

These shows pretend to be kids' cartoons, making you think they're innocent. You might not realize that an adult created and directed these kids' shows. I'll stop here so you can consider it.

Be careful about what influences your children's minds. Always speak positively to your kids. Sow seeds of hope, success, and health in them, and watch those seeds grow into trees that bear fruit.

Instruments

Where have all the instruments gone? Do schools still teach students how to play instruments and read music?

When I was in school, students used to walk around with their flutes, saxophones, trombones, and clarinets. Fast-forward to today, and all I see are kids wearing headphones, listening to cRAP music.[8]

I see a lot of young men trying to become rappers and live that lifestyle. But if we think about it logically, you can only name a hundred, maybe two hundred people who have succeeded in rap.

Think about it: only 100 to 200 people have made it in rapping. There are millions of us here in America. The chances of becoming a rap star are slim. Nobody is offering scholarships for rap. There are plenty of scholarships for musicians.

Instruments broaden our minds. Being able to play an instrument also shows discipline, something that cRAP music doesn't teach.

Children should begin learning to play an instrument early in life. Instead of giving them a phone and headphones, encourage them to learn to play an instrument.

Providing your children with an instrument will help secure their future and expand their creativity. I'd assume that most parents want their children's future to be bright. Instruments are instrumental in doing so.

---

[8] Green, Cliff. "cRAP Music". *Order Over Chaos*, 2024, pp 86 - 87

Money

How much money is enough? In today's world, can you ever truly have enough? What amount would make you feel at ease? Does having money provide you with comfort? Have you achieved your financial goals?

Sometimes, I feel that being at the bottom is better than being at the top. When you're at the bottom, you have something to strive for, goals to reach, people to meet, and a world to conquer.

When you're at the top, you have everything you need. What more could you want? What else can you accomplish? What more can money do for you when you owe nothing and everything's paid off? Besides making sure your family and friends are taken care of, what else can money provide? You might go on more trips, I guess. But what else?

Are people with more money happier? I'm not trying to discourage you from making money because I am still working toward my financial goals. Ultimately, money doesn't define you. Earn money and use it for something positive.

Don't let money control your every thought, but do think of creative ways to earn money.

War Ready

In today's world, you should always be ready for conflict anytime. Some mentally ill people are out there. I train almost every day to be war-ready. After reading this story, I hope it motivates you to do the same.

One time, I was on the metro when this guy got on, and from the moment he entered, I could tell his vibe was off. My instincts told me to keep an eye on him. He walked into the car, turned left toward where I was sitting, then turned right to go in the opposite direction, as if he didn't like the seats on my side. His pace was unusual, and he seemed pretty strange, but he wasn't bothering me or anyone else until he reached the end of the car.

I glanced at my phone for a second, and when I looked up again, he had thrown a woman's luggage on the floor. Then, he sat down next to her.

I'm thinking, OK, are they together and just arguing? You're probably wondering how I could have thought they were together. As I mentioned in my previous books, D.C. has some absolute nutcases.

It turns out they weren't together because the lady tapped the man behind her to ask for help. He told the guy, "Quit tripping, you're acting crazy right now!" He got irate and stood up as if he wanted to fight. So the man who had spoken to him got up too.

He started yelling at him and then told him to do something about it. He called the man a b***h as he stepped off the train—end of story.

Are you ready to fight at a moment's notice? I'm not promoting violence. I'm promoting health, strength, and wellness. What if someone with malicious intent attacked you? Would you be able to defend yourself?

There might not always be someone available to defend you. Therefore, you should always strive to be in top physical condition. We must take proactive steps: work out, exercise, eat healthily, stretch, and practice boxing, martial arts, and other self-defense techniques to protect ourselves, our families, and our loved ones whenever a conflict arises.

Are you war-ready?

Conqueror

If your actions aren't helping you or those around you, it's time to reevaluate them. Our actions should be making us better.

Of course, not every action or step leads to progress because we are all human. We fall and get back up. The problem occurs when we fall and choose to stay down instead of getting back up.

From childhood to adolescence, we make a lot of mistakes from which we should learn. As we become adults, we should grow into well-rounded, functional, and thoughtful individuals. Most adults understand what is right and what is wrong.

The other day, I decided to eat a bag of chips, and I died easily.[9] I'm an adult who chose to eat something that doesn't support my goals.

The decision to eat chips made me take a step back. The crazy thing is that since I have been avoiding eating junk food and cleansing my temple[10] of poisons, toxins, heavy metals, parasites, and harmful organisms; the moment I bit the first chip, my tongue was like, "WTF is this!?!" But I chose to eat them anyway. In that moment, I died easily.

You might be thinking, "Cliff! Chill, it was a bag of chips." But to me, it's more than that. Chips poison my blood. My blood determines how well my manhood

---

[9] Green, Cliff. "Go Hard Or Die Easy". *Less Than a Sack of Weed*, 2020, pp. 40 - 42

[10] Green, Cliff. "Temple". *Order Over Chaos*, 2024, p. 69

rises. Plus, I want to share my best DNA with my lady when it's time for us to have kids.

It's a legacy-building mindset. I challenge myself to achieve and create great things. That moment of weakness slowed my progress just a little.

I try not to let setbacks hold me back for too long! The next day, I put on my sauna top and jumped rope for thirty minutes. Self-improvement has a positive impact on the people around you. Some young men walked by and asked if I boxed. I told them that I didn't box, but I train for life.

I may never know, but I might have shifted their perspective by showing them something constructive and positive.

Now, instead of thinking, "I'm bored. There's nothing to do," they might grab a jump rope and work out. Or they might consider running the steps. When you choose to be the best version of yourself, you create opportunities for others to become the best versions of themselves.

Make sure you create a plan that outlines the steps to reach your goals. Having a clear vision of what you want makes it easier to eliminate unnecessary things.

Remember that your actions must align with your goals. You can go hard or die easy![11] A conqueror will always choose to go hard!

---

[11] Green, Cliff. "Go Hard Or Die Easy". *Less Than a Sack of Weed*, 2020, pp 40 - 42

The Fruits of My Labor

You can't expect rewards if you're not willing to work for them. Don't think that planting a seed in the soil is enough; you have to water and nourish your seed for it to grow. Simply planting an apple seed doesn't guarantee that an apple tree will grow.

You have to nourish your goals like you would a plant. If you neglect nourishing your goals, they will neglect coming to you.

I remember talking to a close friend about what it means to be a genius, and he surprised me with his comment. He said I wasn't a genius, though I am smart, maybe even smarter than most. The only difference between me and others is that I applied myself.

I had to laugh at that because doesn't the act of continually applying myself, even when others choose not to, make me a genius? To apply, by definition, is to make use of something for a specific purpose.

After reading the definition, I see why I am on a path of continuous growth. I've always known I have a purpose. Purpose, by definition, is an intention, aim, or reason for doing something.

Since childhood, I have wanted to accomplish something great. I have used my time, God-given abilities, and mind to reach my goals.

I have achieved a few things, with much more to come. I have reached my goals so far because I am willing to put in the effort. If you reap what you sow, I will enjoy the fruits of my labor.

My friends and others around me have noticed how I've been changing lately. They see my daily efforts to strengthen my mind, body, and soul. They've observed me reading books every day until my mind became as sharp as a katana. They've also noticed positive changes in my eating habits.

They saw me wake up every morning to exercise in the neighborhood. I wasn't running just for my health; I was doing it to positively influence others. I was running for the kid who thinks that Black men only run when they're on a field. I pray that the fruits of my labor fall into the laps of others.

I hope you can say the same. I hope you put in the effort to enjoy the fruits of your labor. Nothing worthwhile comes easily. Make sure to plant your seeds and water them daily.

Reset! Reset! Reset!

Do you remember that friend who always hit the reset button whenever they started losing the game? Nobody liked that kid. If that kid were you, I still hate you! I'm joking, but sometimes I wish life was like Nintendo, and I could hit the reset button whenever I make bad decisions.

That's where my problem is. Everyone treats life like a game, but I'm honest and fair. I am a sincere person who says what I mean. I can't say that's true for everyone I meet.

Let me hit the reset button and go back to when I first noticed those traits in you that I knew I didn't want around me, but I chose to ignore my gut. Now, I have to deal with your nonsense.

That's what I get for ignoring my intuition. When you break the law, you face the consequences. I broke the law by not listening to the Most High when spoken to.

Reset! Reset! Reset!

Can I try again? My life isn't a Nintendo game; I don't have time to play around. If necessary, my circle[12] will get smaller. That's unlikely because I have plenty of real friends. I will be more efficient and avoid people who don't share the same goals, ambitions, and values.

---

[12] Green, Cliff. "Dedication". *Order Over Chaos*, 2024

Reset! Reset! Reset!

This is level one! Are you leveling up with me, or should I unplug your controller?

This Page isn't Working

Consistency pays off. When I blogged, I made sure to post at least once a week. I stuck to my schedule and rarely strayed from it. The only time I didn't blog was when I had internet or computer problems. Something always tries to distract you from your goals. It's natural because what would life be without obstacles?

I remember not being able to post for two weeks because I couldn't log in or access my site at all. Every time I tried to log in, I kept seeing the same message: "This page isn't working."

I read all the articles and watched all the YouTube videos to solve the problem, but to no avail. When I called my hosting provider, they told me that one of my plugins was causing the issue. The representative tried to explain how to fix the problem, but her solution wasn't feasible since my site was down. I was completely locked out of my site.

I used to post a blog every Wednesday. Strangely, something always went wrong with my site or internet connection on those days. Why did I have trouble on Wednesdays? It never failed.

At least once every few months, something happened that made it nearly impossible for me to post. I find it odd and amusing that something always seems to interfere whenever people share transformative information.

I was so focused during the weeks leading up to my page crashing that a bump in the road suddenly appeared. As I typed this, it hit me: bumps in the road are there to slow you down.

If you drive too fast over them, you could seriously damage your vehicle and hurt yourself. Maybe I was speeding and needed to slow down to reassess my direction.

I received several warning signs that made me reevaluate my heart and mind. I ended up fasting and doing a full-body detox. It was a raw food detox, during which I abstained from meat, animal products, and junk food. I also avoided all forms of media. I don't watch TV, but I do enjoy movies and YouTube videos, so I decided to refrain from them too.

My goal was to control my body and mind. I focused on boosting my concentration, determination, and willpower. Detoxing helped me become more in tune with the Most High and myself. I wanted to be so mentally strong that I could send messages telepathically across the country and around the world.

I wanted to break free from relying on the internet. I truly believe humans can communicate telepathically. We have been misled and forgotten our true ways. That's why I shifted from blogging to writing books.

A book can be preserved forever. Blogs and websites can be deleted with a click of a button. The knowledge I have shared can be passed down for generations to come.

Health Over Everything

I'm a health enthusiast who believes in Health Over Everything. I try to gather as much information as I can about health. I have a slim, athletic build because I stretch and work out constantly. I do my best to eat and drink healthily.

I do not follow the Standard American Diet (S.A.D.) because it is detrimental to our health. It's clear that obesity, illnesses, and diseases are at record levels. These issues stem from the food we consume.

On the outside, I appear to be a symbol of health, but despite all my efforts, I realized I wasn't as healthy as I thought.

When I decided to take control of my health, my first step was a 20-day raw food detox. This detox opened my eyes to my unhealthy habits and showed me how much more work I need to do to reach optimal health.

A detox should be the first step for anyone looking to realign their health. This might be a lot of information, but as I mentioned earlier, I have a slim and athletic build. Given that, how was I able to release so many toxins from my body through bowel movements during the detox? I went to the bathroom three, four, five, and sometimes six times a day. I kept asking myself, "Where is all this coming from?"

I lost weight. Huh! You're already slim, Cliff! How could you lose any more weight? I don't know, but it happened. If someone who is already slim and "healthy" can shed so many pounds of waste from their body, how much waste is being stored in the average American's body?

From childhood to early adulthood, I must admit that I was guilty of eating S.A.D.ly, and I faced the consequences[13] of my decisions until I learned to eat better.

Our health is our responsibility, but society has caused us to trust man more than God. People often seek doctors before seeking the Most High. The Most High has given us everything we need to stay healthy and perform our best here on earth.

Mother Nature offers a wide variety of fruits, vegetables, minerals, and herbs for us to enjoy, yet we often choose man-made "food" instead of natural options. Then we wonder why we're all sick. We must realize that man-made food is poisoning us. It gets worse when we rely on a doctor who prescribes a magic pill that masks the problem but never truly fixes it.

This wasn't written to criticize anyone. Everyone has faced health issues. My aim with this chapter is to help you see your health in a new way.

Find a qualified herbalist who can help you with a herbal detox. Choose a detox that cleanses your major organs. Don't treat your car better than you treat your body. Your car gets scheduled maintenance. You

---

[13] Green, Cliff. "Blessings Disguised as a Curse". *Less Than a Sack of Weed*, 2020, pp. 9 - 11

change its oil and flush its fluids. Your body needs that same level of attention. Prioritize your health as much as you prioritize car maintenance.

Learn how to detox. There are so many benefits to detoxing. Remember that you only have one body![14] Please take care of it!

---

[14] Green, Cliff. "You Only Have One Body". *Order Over Chaos*, 2024, pp. 18 - 19

Be tREAL

In the previous chapter, I discussed the necessity of detoxing and its physical benefits. But I did not cover the mental and spiritual advantages of detoxing from electronics.

As we all know, life can be hectic! We try our best with the time we have. Detoxing helps us regain that time. When I detox, I step back from social media, anime, and music as well. This kind of detox may be more difficult than detoxing from food.

We've been conditioned to believe we always need to watch or listen to something. Most people can't even go to the bathroom without their phones. They're addicted to them, even if they don't see it as such. It's an addiction whether you realize it or not, and for that reason alone, everyone should consider a digital detox.

When I decided to live without a TV at 25, I became 25, Black, and Alive (the title of my first blog). I was living in the truest sense of the word. Some magical things started happening to me. I became the creator I am today. My focus sharpened, and I had more time to build my brand.

With TV no longer occupying my thoughts, I had to find other ways to pass the time. That's when I started making jewelry and writing. The **A tREAL O.G**. series is a result of doing digital detoxes.

I remember working a 12-hour shift, then going home, making bracelets, organizing my house, and relaxing with my lady. I ended the night by writing a story. I did all of that before midnight.

I don't think I could do as much if I went home, sat on the couch, and watched TV. I understand why we do it, because our jobs wear us out! Some days, we just want to come home and relax.

We should always make time to rest and relax, but it should be time spent away from watching TV or videos. They offer temporary relief but don't solve the real problem.

Ask yourself: Am I happy with my body? Am I satisfied with my job? Am I financially stable? Am I where I want to be in life? If you answered no to any of these, detoxing from TV and social media might help you.

Videos can be enjoyable, but most don't help you reach your goals. There are definitely videos with great content, but you need to focus entirely on yourself. Work towards achieving things that will improve your situation.

When we limit external influences on our minds, we start to draw from our internal resources. With enough time, our minds will work through and resolve our problems. So, take a break from your phone and TV screen. I promise you'll gain more clarity.

Focus on yourself and don't let anything distract you from your goals.

Stick to the Plan

Everything is as it should be. If it happened, it happened for a reason. Whether it was good or bad, there is a lesson to be learned.

A significant lesson I've learned is to adhere to the plan. Never stray from it. You can adjust the plan, but you must not deviate from it.

Envision your plan. Write it down[15] on paper. Read your plan aloud every day, throughout the day. Then execute your plan.

My plan since I was a kid has always been to become an entrepreneur. But I let outside influences persuade me to attend college, get a good job[16], party, and all the other nonsense people tell you to do, so that you can be stuck like them.

Boy oh boy! I wish I had been this wise when I was that young. That is my goal with these books. Imagine a 14-year-old kid reading and implementing what I said in the previous chapter. They will achieve their goals earlier than most people.

Our goal as parents or elders is to help young people achieve their objectives in half the time it takes us. We should instill in them the value of planning. A person without a plan is a lost individual.

---

[15] Green, Cliff. "The Keys to Success". *Order Over Chaos*, 2024, pp. 90 - 91

[16] Green, Cliff. "Free Game". *Order Over Chaos*, 2024, pp. 43 - 46

Kids Deserve Better

What has happened to protecting your kids from adult topics? I've noticed that a lot of parents lack discretion. They let their children to listen to and watch anything.

Watching TV with your children does not equal screening it for their viewership and safety. Ninety percent of what's on TV is trash. Most television shows consist of nothing but drama-filled entertainment, showcasing a group of confused individuals promoting a message of confusion.

We wonder why our boys and girls are acting out in school and in life. I'm going to take a chance and say that TV makes it seem like drama and foolishness pay off.

There aren't many shows that teach children that being highly educated and intellectual far outweigh being ignorant.

I know many believe that listening to music is harmless, but frankly, it's not. Much of today's music is highly destructive and fosters a spirit of destruction within us.

Read the chapter cRAP Music[17] in Order Over Chaos. Recognize that repetition fosters normalcy. Those in power consistently promote low-quality music, aware that its repetitive messages will embed themselves in the listener's psyche.

---

[17] Green, Cliff. "cRAP Music". *Order Over Chaos*, 2024, pp. 86 -87

More young children have cell phones and headphones. Consider what you can access online. There are some positive aspects, but there are also many negative ones. Imagine a ten-year-old boy who is addicted to pornography. I can assure you that this is occurring at an alarming rate.

We have allowed young people to listen to music and watch whatever they want, whenever they want. When I'm on the metro, there are always kids with headphones on, bobbing their heads or outright dancing. There is nothing wrong with dancing and expressing oneself. There is something wrong when a person isn't expressing[18] themselves but instead is imitating the art[19] they're listening to, looking like an off-brand rapper.

I'm from an era where parents sat down with their kids and reviewed their homework together. Let's reinforce the concept of intellectualism. We need to start now because tomorrow's leaders are formed today. And by today's standards, the future leaders all look tRAPped.

Kids deserve better!

---

[18] Green, Cliff. "EXPRESS Yourself". *Less Than a Sack of Weed*, 2024, pp. 48 - 49

[19] Green, Cliff. "Art". *Order Over Chaos*, 2024, pp. 4 - 5

My Environment

The environment is defined as the surroundings or conditions in which a person, animal, or plant lives or operates.

Most Black people, though not all, would describe the environment where they grew up as "the hood." When you think of the hood, you usually picture a place where violence is common, houses are abandoned, streets are littered, fathers are absent, crime rates are high, gangs are active, and other negative images come to mind.

Whether we like it or not, all of those negative perceptions contain some truth about what is happening in our communities. The question is whether the environment is causing these negatives, or if our minds shape our reality.

We are not products of our environment; instead, our environment is a product of our minds. Our minds shape our reality.

For example, a cluttered mind is more likely to litter. Does the environment cause people to litter, or is it their mindset? It is their mindset that leads to littering, and now they have added more negativity to their surroundings.

If I walk down the street right now, I'll see a neighborhood on the verge of destruction. The issue resides in the minds and hearts of the people. Their hearts have been hardened[20].

If we want our environment to improve, we must change our mindset. We need to remove our blindfolds and perceive reality as it truly is. We must see and think clearly. We should prioritize Order Over Chaos.

It's time for us to free our minds from all negative influences that keep us trapped in a "hood" mentality. If we truly want our community, our children, and our future to thrive, we must adopt a mindset that enables these goals to become a reality.

Be the change you want to see in your environment. Start by cleaning up your front yard, then expand your efforts to clean up the block. It's a monkey see, monkey do[21] world. Nobody wants to be outshined. You could inspire your neighbors to follow suit. Think about launching an initiative to clean up the block. All it takes is one person to make a difference.

Please don't wait until someone else comes to clean up the hood, because once they do that, it's the beginning of the end. Gentrification is occurring across America. Don't let it happen in your neighborhood. Act now!

Your mind has the power to change the world.

---

[20] Green, Cliff. "Hardened Hearts". *Less Than a Sack of Weed*, 2020, pp. 21 - 24

[21] Green, Cliff. "Monkey See, Monkey Do!". *Order Over Chaos*, 2020, pp. 70 - 71

Good Head

Mmm... I love a woman who has a good head on her shoulders. Oh, you thought I was going to be nasty. Did you forget that I'm here to make you think? I'm an intellectual.

I see intelligence as the most attractive trait in people. I enjoy engaging in stimulating conversations that go beyond mundane, everyday topics. A person's intellect resonates more with me than anything else.

Small talk is frustrating because there are too many serious issues to address. I want to figure out how we will overcome our debt, end all meaningless wars, discover The Most High, explore the universe, and heal diseases; you know, the everyday conversations of a wise person.

If everyone raised their frequency, the problems that affect this world would disappear instantly. It's as simple as sharing knowledge with others.

Social media allows us to spread light and truth to everyone. But when I scroll through my timeline, I get bombarded with nonsense. It saddens me to think about it. Honestly, most shows and sports are just distractions, and I can see that people are distracted by what they post.

I've noticed that people only care about important issues when the media brings them up. For example, when a Black boy is unjustly killed, suddenly everyone becomes an activist. That's a problem. People tend to react instead of taking action beforehand.

We can stop all the unnecessary deaths of our people by sharing knowledge. Knowledge can teach our young men how to act accordingly. Knowledge will encourage people to eat healthy and avoid unnecessary illnesses and early death.

Some people are dissatisfied with their current circumstances and the events in their lives. Knowledge can help solve their problems. The drugs, alcohol, and entertainment only mask the pain and temporarily distract us.

We must face life with sobriety and a sound mind. If everyone had a good head on their shoulders, we would be able to help one another by sharing our experiences and trials. Your experiences may help the next person overcome their obstacles.

Let's hold each other accountable. Let's invest more in developing our minds. When we do, our community and country will thrive. I hope you find a tribe full of people with good heads on their shoulders before the great reset.

No Hookups

Support the people you know, like you support those you don't. If you have a friend or family member who sells clothes, don't ask them for a freebie. Support their effort and buy a shirt or two.

Share their content on social media as if it were your own. Present it as if it were a product of a celebrity. Support the people you know and care about, or should I say, "that you say you care about."

You've never been to Walmart and asked for a free shirt. So why do you ask your friends, who are trying to run profitable businesses, for free stuff?

We need to stop approaching each other looking for handouts. There is no longer any "Let me get a hookup" going on. Instead, we should be asking how we can help our friends succeed and flourish.

I've observed that every community is growing businesses and developing technologies to advance themselves. They prioritize family above everything else and support one another.

Honestly, there's nothing wrong with that. This isn't to say you can't support other cultures and their businesses. We need to support and rebuild our own families before focusing on helping others.

This is, in fact, how the world operates. The Black man and woman forgot the code and became lost along the way.

There are no more handouts. You should genuinely care about what your loved one is creating. If a product or service is lacking, avoid supporting low-quality businesses. Instead, offer some constructive feedback to help them improve.

Y2K

If phones, laptops, and computers suddenly stopped working, would you be able to survive? What if grocery stores ran out of food or stopped selling it; would you be able to eat?

Can you hunt? Can you garden? More importantly, have you been gardening? You can't plant a seed today and expect a meal tomorrow. Plants require time to grow.

Can you read a map? Do you know how to use a compass? Can you start a fire without a lighter? Do you have an emergency kit?

Are you healthy enough to walk to a family member's house? A family member who might reside in the next town over.

I am not trying to scare you because no one knows what may or may not happen.

This is an exercise in self-reflection. I want you to be proactive, not reactive. I prefer that you are prepared rather than having to get prepared.

Train Trappin' (Part 1)

I could write an entire book about my experiences on the metro. There's never a dull moment on the train.

One day, someone might be screaming at the top of their lungs for no apparent reason. The next day, another person would walk up to every single passenger and ask for 17 cents. Yes, 17 cents. There are days when not much happens. It's just the usual loud and obnoxious teenagers acting foolishly—nothing out of the ordinary.

I remember a time when I was sitting there, minding my own business, when two boys began play fighting behind me. I'm used to that. As a teenager, I slap-boxed and wrestled with my friends.

But you know how to recognize who will cause problems and who won't? Well, the one I anticipated would be trouble was the one creating all the commotion.

He punched the other boy and ran off the train while the other chased him. They brushed against my shoulder as they left. Nothing major, but one of the girls with them said, "So you're just going to run into that man like that? I'm sorry, sir. I'll apologize for them."

After she said that, I asked her and the group if they were tired of seeing Black boys die. Naturally, they all said yes. I then inquired if I should respect boys acting like their friends. They all replied no. Next, I asked whether White people should respect boys acting like their friends do. Again, they all said no. I posed one last question: What do you all think will keep happening to our young men if they continue to act this way? The young lady responded that they would keep being killed.

Because she impressed me so much, I gave her $20. Then, after asking the group who was the smartest, I gave the other four $20 to split among themselves. I told them that people are rewarded for doing good, positive, and bright things.

As they got off the train, I made sure they told their friends what had happened. Two of them got off with me, and I told the young man that I could see he had a vision and wanted to achieve things in his life. I advised him never to let his environment take that away from him. Keep your grades up and focus on everything you want to pursue. Then, I gave him and the girl he was with another $10.

How can we change the narrative? How can we encourage our youth to behave positively? One of the first things we can do is show them that there are older individuals who genuinely care about their well-being.

The five kids were old enough and smart enough to remember what happened to them that day—the day an older Black man showed them love. What if more of our men began doing that every day? It doesn't always have to be with money; it can also be words of encouragement.

In "Which came first, the chicken or the egg?" I asserted that the elders have let down our youth. We must restore the wisdom that was entrusted to us.

Trap some youth into achieving greatness.

48

Train Trappin' (Part 2)

You have to experience riding the D.C. metro. I remember the day five young men got on the train. They acted foolishly, to the point that I felt I had to say something.

I called them over and asked a few questions. I inquired if they had noticed what the police were doing to young Black men. One boy kept asking if I was a cop. I had to explain that I wasn't, but he was fixated on the idea that I was. I didn't understand why until he pointed at my bag and asked what the logo meant.

He was very observant. He noticed that my bag had " tactical " in its name. I explained to him that it was simply the name on my bag and that I wasn't a cop.

I told them that the police have been acting like demons towards us for some time and that there is no need to give them further reasons to continue their demonic behavior.

They got the picture, but to ensure I wasn't just preaching to them, I asked them how many of them there were. They said, "Five. " Okay, if I give you $25, how much would each of you get? They replied, "FIVE!" with quickness. Word, so you're good at math.

I gave them $25 and told them to split it accordingly. Then I explained that I wouldn't be able to give money to them if I wasn't focused, and they wouldn't be able to do the same if they didn't learn how to focus.

As we stepped off the train, one of them was shadowboxing. I said, "Oh, you box?" He replied, "Yup! And I'm about to go pro." I asked him where they train, and he told me at Tony's gym. I still haven't found the time to visit him, but I hope my words resonated with them.

I wrote this chapter to emphasize the importance of being in the streets and teaching our young men. A lot of them aren't receiving this guidance at home.

We can't preach to kids. Especially kids who really don't want to hear us. They want to see the rewards. Since all they hear in music is trap this and trap that, we need to work harder to show them there are other options.

The War on Women

Take a moment to watch Dr. Llaila Afrika's lecture on fibroids on YouTube. He discusses the issues and offers information on healing various women's problems.

I know several women who have shared with me their experiences related to their wombs—issues like fibroids and cysts. They explained that when they visited the doctor, the doctor's primary course of action was to remove the ovaries and uterus.

Doctors promote hysterectomies for women as if they are the solution. They understand that we have been conditioned to view the doctor as the ultimate authority, but the reality is that many doctors are unethical and motivated by profit. This is why they employ scare tactics when interacting with patients.

The Most High put us here to procreate. So, why do doctors insist on removing the things that women need to have babies? Mmm... It sounds devilish to me. It seems like population control. It feels like war.

Let's not overlook that abortion and birth control are intentionally promoted in non-white communities.

Please take a moment to look up Margaret Sanger and watch some of her clips. You might be surprised by what you hear.

Damn! Did you cringe a little while listening to her? You should have. She was nothing short of evil. Oh! And a lady politician has proclaimed her to be a hero. While her husband was locking up Black men so they couldn't father Black children. Sounds like war to me.

It is time we see and understand that our existence here has faced resistance. Resistance that prefers to see us in the ground, not above it. A resistance that doesn't want us to have children.

Cutting out the womb is an act of war! It is a war on women and a war against God.

The Spark

A clear mind leads to a clear soul, and a clear soul and mind contribute to a healthy body. When all three—mind, body, and soul—harmonize, we become whole or (w)holy.

A strong mind yearns for a strong soul, and a strong soul longs for a strong body in which to reside. A strong mind recognizes the importance of nurturing the body to maintain healthy, robust blood. A healthy mind will always possess that spark.

Sometimes, I contemplate a single idea, but a seemingly unrelated connection ignites in my mind and suddenly makes complete sense.

For instance, when I was searching for trucks, I came across one with manual windows. Suddenly, an unsettling thought struck me: how many Black men might have been shot by police simply for having to roll down their windows manually?

Let's create a quick story. A police officer stops a young Black man for a routine traffic stop. As he approaches the car, he notices the man leaning slightly and reaching down. The officer can a) assume he is rolling down his window, b) reaching for a weapon, or c) discarding something. We all know they have been trained to perceive Black men as a threat.

Now the cop claims to be nervous and reaches for his weapon before knowing what the young man is doing. Bang! Another one down because the cop said he "feared for his life. " That is all he needs to say to justify his actions.

That may seem morbid. You might ask me, "Why did you think about something so dark when you were just looking for a truck?" My answer is, "The Spark." The spark enables you to connect the dots where they usually aren't connected.

Do you see how one thought sparked another in my mind? Everyone has these abilities. I hope to inspire you to unlock your mind's full and true potential.

I want everyone to feel the spark. The spark connects the past, present, and future, enabling you to create connections where many people struggle. It empowers you to function at a higher level.

At our core, we all want to operate at our highest level and reach our full potential. The best thing you can do is take care of your health.

The healthier you are, the better your blood flows to your brain. Your brain requires oxygen and blood flow to function optimally, and blood and oxygen deliver essential nutrients.

Even as I sit here editing this book, a revelation has come to me. In "Family Equals Perfection[22]" I discussed how we carry information in our DNA from the beginning. The idea of possessing pure blood may evoke thoughts of an ancestor in your mind.

You possess powers that lie dormant within you! I hope I've ignited your passion to release them!

---

[22] Green, Cliff. "Family Equals Perfection". *Less Than a Sack of Weed*, 2020, pp. 96 - 99

High Expectations

I truly expect a lot from myself! I hope that by the end of this chapter, you hold high expectations for yourself as well.

I have friends, family, and associates who expect a great deal from me. I can't let myself or them down. High expectations bring many responsibilities, which can sometimes feel burdensome.

In the Bible, Luke 12:48 says, "To whom much is given, much is required." Aww man, I probably scared off some super-conscious people by referencing the Bible. Lol.

The Most High has bestowed gifts, talents, and intelligence upon everyone, yet very few people utilize their gifts to their full potential. I have chosen to be among the small percentage of individuals who do. I am writing this in the hope of awakening your latent abilities.

Again, we all have them. I remember my friend Gary from college calling himself E.D.O.T., which stood for Every Drop of Talent. I admired his confidence. Even though I haven't spoken to him in a while, I know he is on a path toward greatness. He recognized early in life that he was blessed with gifts, and he wasn't afraid to show them.

Read that last sentence once more. He wasn't afraid to show them. Fear is one of the key differences between doers and non-doers.

Once I let go of my fear, I grew tremendously. Working through situations that you fear or find uncomfortable helps you grow as a person. I'll admit that being uncomfortable can be frightening.

But who has time to be scared? I could have stayed in the hood and been comfortable, chilling with people doing things that weren't helping me, my family, or my community.

But I knew that so much was expected of me. People expect me to succeed and break barriers, to inspire and lead others towards greatness. I've come to place these expectations on myself because I demand so much of myself.

What standards do you have? What expectations do you have for yourself? If no one is there to push you, will you push yourself?

I cannot let The Most High, my family, or my friends down. And neither should you!

Difference of Opinion

To reinforce the ideas from previous chapters about having gifts and abilities, would you believe that I freestyled this chapter on my phone?

My brother and I debated whether calling out Black people for their missteps was negative. He thought it was, while I disagreed. I suppose we have differing opinions.

We must address the problems, or they won't be resolved. He believes that the news does an excellent job of highlighting our missteps, and I concur. The news goes above and beyond to emphasize every unfortunate incident in our culture.

But the news only highlights mishaps. It doesn't address the root of the issue. It will persist until the problem is corrected at its core.

Perhaps I should have begun this chapter with my statement that led him to accuse me of being negative. In a group thread among brothers, I stated, "We (Black people) as a whole have a negative mentality."

He replied that we don't respond well to things like that. So, what do we respond to? Why should we gloss over everything and make it sound like peaches and cream when we all know it isn't?

As I mentioned earlier, littered minds lead to littered environments. Most communities where we live collectively are filled with waste. Litter doesn't simply appear. Trash in your mind results in trash around you, and that's where we stand as a society.

Someone else mentioned in the group that we have a crab-like mentality. I write and express my thoughts with the hope that someone might read or hear them and look in the mirror, realizing, "Damn! I was doing that. I didn't even realize what I was doing was wrong. I'm going to change that."

Even though my friend and I have differing opinions, we both understand our ultimate goal. We do not intend to let minor differences hinder us.

That brings me to another point that needs to be addressed within our community. We let minor differences prevent us from seeing the bigger picture and working together.

A man could have done and said a million things right that would benefit us, but if he falters even once, all faith is lost.

History has conditioned us to believe that we need a perfect leader. We have been waiting for him to descend from the heavens for years. This is not intended as a criticism of Christians; rather, it serves as a wake-up call.

God has granted you the ability, light, energy, and intellect to guide yourself and make meaningful decisions. He didn't instruct us to sit idly and wait indefinitely. How does the verse go? "Faith without works is dead."

We are in a time when the divine within you seeks to connect with the divine within others. To achieve this connection, we must rise above minor differences hindering our progress toward the greater good of our community and humanity.

That should be something we can all agree on. Right? Can we build even with our minor differences?

Feelings

Can I share a time when I was experiencing an emotional funk? I had just broken up with my ex, and honestly, I was struggling. It took some serious introspection to realize that many funks are self-imposed. We bring them upon ourselves through our thoughts and actions.

Even though I was going through it, I refused to fall into a negative cycle. I decided to dedicate my time to improving myself. I focused on my goals and used that emotional energy as fuel to level up. I knew I had dragged myself into that funk, so naturally, I had to find a way to get out of it.

One of the best things a person can learn is to master their emotions. Take responsibility for your mistakes. Don't allow your feelings to lead you into irrational actions. Find productive ways to occupy your time. Reflect on your mistakes and learn from them. If you can achieve this, you will become a force to be reckoned with.

Please don't let this chapter or any of my other books confuse you, as I am a work in progress. I do not have all the answers. I share my problems and solutions in these books to help those experiencing similar situations.

Keep working on improving yourself spiritually, mentally, and physically. Learn to view obstacles as lessons. Recognize that pain serves a purpose. Learn

from it and grow because of it. It will only hold you back
if you let it.

The Golden Rule

You cannot expect people to listen to you if you don't listen to them. Regardless of what the other person is saying, no one enjoys a one-sided conversation. It makes them feel that the person couldn't care less about their input, leading them to think they shouldn't care about the other person's opinions.

James 1:19 states, "My dear brothers and sisters, take note of this: Everyone should be quick to listen, slow to speak, and slow to anger." I wish I had heeded these words much earlier in life, but we live, learn, and hopefully grow.

The Golden Rule is to treat others as you would like to be treated. Matthew 7:12 states, "So in everything, do to others what you would have them do to you..."

If you want others to hear what you have to say, you must also be humble enough to listen to them.

Listening intently to people will enable you to dissect their words. If warranted, you can then provide your input. Remember that not everyone seeks a response; some are simply looking for a listening ear. By listening closely, you can discern the type of conversation you're having.

Try not to be a "do as I say, not as I do " person. It can be challenging to uphold your ideals when your head is in the clouds, but setting an example is important. Actions speak louder than words.

The Golden Rule will bring you mental, physical, spiritual, and financial prosperity. Who would turn down gold if it were offered to them?

Make It Happen

I remember telling my cousin Donald (may he rest in peace) that I wanted to write a book, and he advised me to start a blog first. I took his advice, and here we are now. This is the third installment of **A tREAL O.G.** Because I expressed my intention to write a book, I had to follow through and write one.

When I consistently blogged every Wednesday, I felt overwhelmed trying to balance my blog and work schedules.

The schedule was crazy. I started work at 3 p.m. on Monday. I got to my destination around midnight. I would stay at that destination all day on Tuesday. Then, I would go to work at 4 a.m. on Wednesday. After work, I would get home around 3 p.m., then meet my brother Rob to work out or hoop.

I had the same schedule on Friday. There were days I would get in at midnight, then wake up at 5:00 a.m. on Saturday and run a couple of miles with my brothers. Afterward, I worked on my house.

The schedule had me away from my apartment so often that I was mad about still having to pay rent. The days I spent at home were filled with household chores.

By the time I got home on Wednesday evenings, I was exhausted. All I wanted to do was sleep, but I had to blog. I considered changing my blog post day to Thursdays.

Even though that would've alleviated some pressure, I couldn't do it. When I first started blogging, I promised myself and others that I would post every Wednesday.

The moral of this story is to be consistent and to keep your word. Your word is your bond. If you say it, do it! Or are you lying to yourself and others?

Read the Preface of Less Than a Sack of Weed, and you will understand how dedication and consistency have paid off. You are witnessing the fruits of consistency and the importance of meaning what you say. You have the power to do the same.

Imagine consistently creating something every week. Within a year, you would have 52 creations. These can be assembled for sale or admiration. Either way, the joy of creating is worth more than money. Witnessing your mind's work come to life will also boost your confidence.

Passion & Purpose

Without passion, you're basically a zombie. Passion gives us purpose. Passion is a strong liking, desire, or dedication to a specific activity, object, or idea. A lot of books on success describe passion as a burning desire or a flame within that drives you toward what you love.

America has trained us to view success solely in monetary terms, but financial success does not always equate to happiness and joy. The only time financial success brings happiness is when it is attained by someone following their passion.

Nothing makes a person feel better than pursuing their passions. Would I be wrong to say that I believe most Americans have allowed their inner fire to dim?

This may explain why Americans face a high rate of depression. Many individuals work jobs they dislike and then return home to watch TV. Television often worsens their depression, as it seems that most people on screen are pursuing their passions, which fosters feelings of inadequacy in viewers.

To free ourselves from the daily monotony, we must detach from distractions. Find a quiet room in your home and reflect. Recall when you were a child or a teenager, filled with vivid dreams. Dreams that bring a smile to your face when you remember them.

What were those dreams about? What about them makes you smile? What did you dream of being? Who did you dream of becoming? After you think about all of that, write everything down. Write out your dreams, both old and new.

Then, take ten minutes out of your day, every day, to do what makes you smile. Those ten minutes will turn into twenty. The twenty minutes will turn into thirty. And so on. Before you know it, your entire day will be filled with living in your passion.

I'm not telling you what to do like a controlling parent; I'm engaging with you as I share what I've learned. My passion has always been helping others. If even one of my books has changed someone's life, I have fulfilled my purpose.

My passion is so intense that when I don't immediately see the fruits of my labor, it can be disheartening. I know I have changed this world because people have told me so, but I need to see more results because I'm passionate about helping people.

That's how you should live and feel. Allow that desire to burn deep within you and never let your fire dwindle. It will reward you in more ways than one.

White Excuses

There is a system actively trying to oppress Black people, but I still watch those who blame everything on White Supremacy. Those people might be agents sent to distract us from the real issues.

I'm not saying that White people haven't committed atrocities against us, and I'm not suggesting that you shouldn't keep a watchful eye on them. Nor am I implying that every single one of them is a bad person. What I'm saying is that it's time to focus on fixing ourselves and building together for one another.

The problems faced by the Black community won't be solved until we confront them head-on. For example, the other day, while I was riding the subway, a young woman sat right in front of me, opened some candy, and then threw the wrappers on the floor. Did a White person make her litter?

I am in the hood every day, whether it's my neighborhood in Pittsburgh or where I live in D.C. The other day, while I was back home cleaning up the street, I saw a 40-oz bottle on the curb along with some other trash. I can't lie, I instantly got irritated.

Let me explain why. In D.C., the number of Black men who walk around in a drunken stupor is shocking. I recall passing by some not too long ago and hearing one of them say that the White man is the reason they are down.

I thought to myself that the White man isn't forcing you to drink. The White man isn't forcing you to throw all your beer cans and bottles on the ground. He's not forcing you to hang outside the liquor store like it's your best friend's house.

I could walk around the corner right now and take a picture of nine Black men sitting in lawn chairs outside the liquor store owned by Asian men. This raises another point: no one, and I mean no one, cares about our issues, even if White people were responsible for creating them. Everyone else focuses only on building for themselves and protecting their own. They can fight any injustices that come their way.

I am knowledgeable about history and understand that a system exists from which White people benefit.

Yes, there is a system in place working to keep us down. Yes, they put drugs in our communities. Yes, they intentionally broke up our family structure. Yes, the education system is a school-to-prison pipeline. The list of atrocities can go on and on, but what are we doing to fight back?

We need to eliminate divisions among us to build a system that protects and benefits everyone. I've studied hard to understand true history, and I'm dedicated to preventing it from repeating. Also, I've always disliked the term "White Supremacy" because giving another person the label of 'supreme' has never sat well with me.

A Wasteful Society

There will come a time when all the wasteful things happening in America cease.

Let's consider food (if we can truly call it that) as an example. In America, there are 660,775 restaurants combined. At the end of the night, let's say each one of those restaurants throws away just one meal that it couldn't sell. We all know they throw away much more than that, but that still amounts to 660,775 meals wasted in one night.

Couldn't each of those meals be donated to someone in need? If companies are concerned about being sued, they could create a waiver or release form that must be signed to donate their food. This form would protect them from legal action if the person they fed became ill.

Now, let's discuss car companies. All across America, hundreds of cars sit in dealership lots—cars that are unlikely to be sold. Why aren't cars made to order? Why aren't there cars available for customers to test drive? If they are impressed, they could choose to order that specific car.

I don't understand why there needs to be 300 cars in one lot. Where are all the resources coming from? How can we continue producing so many cars each year without depleting resources? Maybe minerals and resources are infinite, and I'm simply ignorant. Still, to me, the entire car industry seems wasteful.

Do you believe we should be mindful of the companies we support? Should we, as individuals, cultivate more seeds to give back to the Earth? How can we live more harmoniously with nature?

I don't have all the answers, but I enjoy sharing my perspective and hopefully inspiring reflection.

Beautiful Murals

In hoods throughout America, murals depict fallen soldiers and people who have lost their lives to senseless violence.

Though the artwork on these murals is beautiful, wouldn't it have been even more stunning if the person depicted on the wall hadn't had their life cut short? They also could have lived out their dreams and pursued their ambitions.

I don't want to see another brother painted on a wall. I want to witness his expressions while he's alive. What must happen for us to show love to one another? How can we stop the hate?

It is troubling when a man can harm another man who resembles his cousin. In my family, we show love to one another. We have disputes and arguments, but we either talk them out or give each other some space.

My goal is to help us see each other as family. I fulfill my role in daily life. I consistently acknowledge a brother or express love in some way, hoping to plant a seed so that the man or woman I show love to will turn around and share that love with someone else.

How can we create a mural of love in each other's hearts? How have you contributed? Make some art and let your light shine on someone!

I Am a Company

Don't get discouraged if your goals aren't materializing quickly. Stay committed to your plan and review your steps carefully. You might have made an error that is hindering your progress.

Once you identify the mistake, think about how you can correct it. Evaluate the lessons learned from your mistakes and strive not to repeat them.

We've all made excuses to justify not reaching our goals. Maybe our job doesn't fit a traditional lifestyle, but we should use that to push ourselves forward. We can choose a different path.

It all comes down to the choices we make. Every decision I've made so far has led me to where I am today. I'm in a good position because I've made solid choices, and my job can be exciting sometimes, but deep down, I know I have much more to offer the world. Making good money while dreading work isn't what I want out of life.

Everyone is here to be their best selves. Most jobs, 9-to-5s, and careers are not designed to help you become your best self. They exist so you can make the company you work for the best it can be. As I write this, I realize I must treat my life like a business.

I am a company, so I need to organize my life as if I were working for someone else. We wake up and go to work on demand for another company. Why not incorporate that same discipline into ourselves?

This chapter acts as a pep talk for both of us. I felt I wasn't completely on my path; thousands of others feel the same. Sometimes, you need to step back, relax, and reflect until the answers come. They will come.

Men Bring Order!

I've been working on my childhood home for some time now. I noticed the house across the street from mine needed some yard work. The man in me immediately wanted to take care of it, but I wasn't sure if the lady lived alone.

Last summer, I almost had the nerve to go over there and do it anyway, but something told me not to. When I returned the next day, I noticed three men standing on the house's walkway.

It struck me: Men must return to being men. The man in me would never allow a lady's house to look so neglected, whether she is a friend, girlfriend, sister, or cousin. I'm highlighting this because these guys know the lady and visit her home, yet none of them were man enough to help with her yard. Men are meant to protect women.

Someone might ask if they lack the tools. What if that's their girlfriend and not their wife? Look, men possess the tools. As stated in the Preface of "Order Over Chaos," men bring order. People can't keep complaining about what's happening in our communities, yet when a man presents a solution, you criticize that, too.

All is well, though. My brother happened to know the lady and informed her that I wanted to trim her bushes and that I would do it for free. She was hesitant at first because things like this don't happen as often as they should in our neighborhoods. I trimmed her bushes and weed-whacked her yard while those other men watched. She was grateful.

I have two reasons for this. First, I want to lead by example. Those guys have now seen what men do. Hopefully, the lady understands how the men around her are expected to act. Second, this is my block, and I will treat it as such.

Hocus Focus

The more I study, the more I understand what it takes to succeed. You have to be able to focus- really concentrate. In today's world, focusing is nearly impossible due to all the distractions around us. It seems almost impossible, but everything is possible, especially when we direct our minds toward our objectives.

The mind is the key to achieving whatever you desire in life. We should fill our minds with things that propel us forward. Anything that doesn't improve you is merely a distraction. And remember, we exist in a world filled with distractions.

The average attention span is similar to that of a fruit fly. This comparison may seem negative, but it highlights the reality of today's world, where we often partake in meaningless activities that do not help us progress.

Our minds can no longer focus on the task without wandering off into the abyss. But now is the time to reprogram. Learn to place your goals at the forefront of your mind. Keep them in your heart. Embed them in your conscious and subconscious mind. Please do not allow them to leave your sight.

Repeat your goals to yourself whenever you can. Recite them when you wake up and before you lay your head down at night. Write them out and place them in visible spots, like on mirrors or refrigerator[23] doors. By doing these things, you will be doing magic on yourself. You will cast a spell that helps you stay focused.

Your goals and objectives will become so deeply embedded in your being that your actions will effortlessly guide you toward achieving them.

---

[23] Green, Cliff. "How to Become More Goal-Oriented". *Less Than a Sack of Weed*, 2020, pp. 29 - 30

Buying Our Worth

I love to dress up and look nice just as much as anyone else, but I have always questioned why I, along with most people in my community, feel this constant need to dress well.

What did Ye say on that track? "I can't even go to the grocery store. Without some one's that's clean and a shirt with a team."

I'm not too proud to admit that there have been many times when I couldn't figure out what I wanted to wear. The sad part is that I wasn't going anywhere special.

Meanwhile, billionaires wear the same T-shirt every day, claiming they don't want to waste precious time and energy on trivial things like choosing clothes. They prefer to spend their time serving their community.

Logically, there isn't any real reason to own more than four or five pairs of shoes: a pair of black shoes, a pair of white shoes, a pair of boots, and a pair of dress shoes. Not long ago, I totaled the money I'd spent on the shoes in my closet, and I felt disgusted. Imagine if all that money spent on shoes went toward something meaningful.

Is fashion innate in Black men and women? Or do we possess a low sense of self-worth, attempting to buy and showcase our worth through clothing and material possessions?

To answer my own question. Fashion isn't a color thing. I have noticed that a lot of young Asian people love to dress nicely. They be dripped up too. But I can't speak for issues that may concern them. I know that in my community, people buy things they can't afford in order to keep up with the Joneses.

Every Single Day!

Every
Single
Day!

There are no days off when you're aiming to accomplish something. If you find yourself taking days off, it might mean you're not fully passionate about what you do.

Over the past few years, I've been renovating a house. It's been a complete renovation, from the basement to the roof, and honestly, I've enjoyed every moment.

I love it so much that sometimes I can't sleep some nights because I'm thinking of ways to build the house. Even if I have to be at work early the next day, I'd rather be at the house working late into the night.

Your goals should ignite a fire within you. They should bring you happiness when you think about them. You should be quietly obsessed with them, but to achieve them, you need to put in the work.

Every
Single
Day

Do your goals keep you up at night? Is there something that sparks a fire in you? If so, you'd better get up and get to it.

Every
Single
Day

Get in Front of Me!

Good parenting versus bad parenting. I remember taking the metro to work when I saw a young mother ignoring her son. The young boy wandered away from his mother. I kept a watchful eye on him while noting how long it took her to realize he was drifting away. She took so long that anyone could have easily run off with her son.

She didn't even notice that her son had wandered off. He went around a wall that was obstructing her view. The only advantage for her was that she was at the metro, and heroes[24] who wouldn't let anything happen to a child? This brings me to the story's point, where I inform her about her young boy's whereabouts.

As I reflect on it, perhaps the young lady sensed the presence of a man nearby, which may have alleviated her fear of anything negative occurring. After all, men are here to protect and provide. I can't assert this was the case, but if it was, kudos to her spirit for being in tune.

I genuinely feel this was more about a young parent acting young, neglecting her responsibilities as a mother. She was more focused on whatever was happening on her phone screen than on her son's whereabouts or activities.

---

[24] Green, Cliff. "Be an Everyday Hero". *Less Than a Sack of Weed*, 2020, pp. 62 - 63

On the opposite side of this story, I passed a young lady around my age walking with her two daughters on my way home. As I walked past, she said to her daughter, "Get in front of me!" That short yet stern sentence brought a smile to my face.

The first lady may have been a wonderful parent, but she experienced a moment of negligence that could have had a serious consequence.

This chapter was not written to diminish her but to raise awareness of our actions—of all our actions as parents and as bystanders. Bystanders were once seen as the village. We must return to our roots!

We have seen millions of news stories about child trafficking. Trafficking is a serious problem plaguing the world. As parents and concerned citizens, we must remain extremely vigilant of our surroundings and keep a watchful eye on our children.

Don't get too Comfortable

To grow, you need to go beyond what you're used to. Comfort can be dangerous. When we become too comfortable, we risk becoming stuck. I'm not talking about the comfort of your bed or sofa. I'm referring to the comfort that happens when you tell yourself you've arrived.

Being too comfortable is a dangerous place to be, even if you've already reached your goals. You woke up this morning, and there's still a lot of work to do. You should keep improving and pushing beyond your limits.

You won't accomplish much if you're too comfortable. That's why I didn't have a couch in my apartment during the first couple of years.

I recently bought a TV to accommodate a guest because I don't usually watch TV. TV creates a false sense of comfort. You come home from work, sit on the couch, and turn on the TV to relax just because you have a comfortable sofa.

This might seem excessive to some, but I don't want to feel comfortable. How can I be comfortable when I'm not where I want to be? I have so much more to accomplish, and the moment I say, "I am good," I will lose my momentum.

I want to evolve into the best version of myself. You should strive to do the same. Never use comfort as an excuse to remain stagnant. Excuses arise from fear. The only thing I fear is complacency.

The Light Within

I went to Jamaica a while back for my birthday. During that time, I took a brief break from writing. Although the trip was relaxing and much needed, I had to get back on my Ps and Qs as soon as I returned to the States.

When I returned, I hit the ground running. I remember witnessing a young man make way for a woman with crutches to exit the metro. I had to speak to that young man. It may sound crazy, but I am delighted to see a young man doing something honorable.

When I caught up, I introduced myself and mentioned that I saw what he did. Then, I handed him the remaining money in my wallet—just over $20. I needed to ensure he understood that his actions were commendable and that he should maintain that same spirit throughout his life.

Later that day, I went to get some food, and the woman who took my order was very friendly. She mentioned that she had just graduated from Pitt and would be heading back home in three weeks. Her homeland was Serbia. She explained how many of her friends were struggling to obtain their green cards and visas due to the policies being enacted. We had a pleasant conversation.

After paying for my sandwich, I gave her a few bucks. She was so ecstatic. She exclaimed, "Are you for real? This much!" I replied, "Yeah! Congratulations on graduating, and happy holidays to you!" Then, I walked out of the store. Thirteen dollars isn't a lot of money, but people don't typically tip at this type of restaurant, and I am a stranger to her. That was completely unexpected.

I was in a retail store. A family was ahead of me at another register, and it seemed they were having difficulty purchasing their items. After buying my item, I helped their daughter stand up after she had fallen.

Then I asked the mother if she would mind if I bought their items as a holiday gift. She looked at me with disbelief, but eventually said Okay. After paying for their items, I shook her son's hand and told him to stay focused. Then I walked out of the store.

Though I know I don't need to shop, perhaps that is why God led me to the store. I could have walked straight into the gym, but something urged me to enter the store instead.

These three stories occurred within a couple of days of each other. I have a thousand more stories like them, all of which I don't have enough time to write. The moral of these stories is that I want to be a beacon of light and hope for others. I want people to know that the Most High exists and that there are individuals out there who genuinely care about the well-being of their fellow humans.

A lot of us work jobs to get by. They may not enjoy what they do, but they maintain a smile and carry out their work with love. Whenever I see the light shining within others, I want to help keep it shining and, if possible, make it brighter.

Spread love to others. Help those in need without expecting anything in return. The benefits far surpass what money can provide.

Avoid sharing every instance of your help to others. Don't do it just for your ego.

You are reading this now because my books aim to share uplifting and inspiring stories. I want to see everyone's light shining!

Quit Lying!

Would telling your kid the truth about holidays make them less of a child? Probably not! How long will we continue to lie to our children? Prayerfully, they will grow wise and seek truth.

People love to fantasize about rising above their struggles. There is nothing wrong with coming from the bottom and rising to the top. I want everybody to reach their max potential, but we need to quit glorifying the struggle.

Thousands of parents are spending money they don't have to provide their children with materials that will likely be disregarded in two weeks. We know that kids change their minds frequently, yet we continue to satisfy all their childish desires.

We should give children opportunities that help them become great thinkers, inventors, and creators. We should be developing business leaders, engineers, inventors, and pioneers.

"But Cliff, you don't have children and don't know what it's like!" You're right. I don't. I do know the difference between right and wrong. I understand the power of the mind and how it should be nurtured toward greatness. I also recognize that providing my children with knowledge safeguards their future and mine.

All I'm saying is that we need to move past the lies. You work hard all year to lie to your child, making them believe that a stranger brought them presents.

You know how hard you have to work to provide for your family. Do you want your kid to have to work the same? If you're going to spend your hard-earned money, you might as well spend it on building your kid's future.

Resolutions

Now is the perfect time to put your best foot forward and declare that this year will be the year you move with clarity.

To maintain a clear vision, try to avoid distractions. Try not to consume anything that can harm our minds and bodies.

Every year on December 31st, millions of people gather at clubs, bars, and social events to celebrate the new year. I hope they enjoy themselves and have a good time. But does their fun come at a cost? Did their enjoyment lead them to their resolutions or set them back a step or two?

I know a lot of people have resolutions to go to the gym and work out more often, which is a great resolution—more power to them. I pray you accomplish all you set out to do.

I'm writing to introduce some new ideas you may not have heard before. The new year isn't actually January 1st; we're using the wrong calendar. Look it up. I share this to help you reach your goals.

Some people will get intoxicated on New Year's Eve. Even if we followed the correct calendar, wouldn't that set the new year off on the wrong foot? Intoxication doesn't lead to a clear mind.

Do you get excessively drunk or high every year? I'm not trying to make you feel guilty; I've been there, grown, and now see things clearly. Once I broke free from that endless cycle, my life improved. I have accomplished more.

It's so much harder to wake up and work out after a night of drinking. Alcohol used to slow me down. It dampened my enthusiasm on some days and made me reluctant to get up and be productive.

We say we want to accomplish things, but hinder ourselves by clinging to old habits. Why start the New Year intoxicated? What's new about that? You should enter the New Year with a clear, sober mind. How will you approach this year differently? Do you want to grow, or do you prefer to stay stuck in your old ways?

These are challenging questions to answer. They require self-reflection and honesty. I've asked this before, and I'm asking you again: "How serious are you?"[25]

If you've been drinking every new year, don't worry about it. You can't change the past, and tomorrow never comes.[26] All we have right now is this moment. Will you resolve to be the best version of yourself?

Plus, your birthday marks the start of your new year. Still, you shouldn't get intoxicated. Birthdays are another topic I plan to explore in a future book.

Will you challenge yourself or take the easy route? The choice is yours. Please choose wisely!

---

[25] Green, Cliff. "You Do Have Something to Prove". *Less Than a Sack of Weed*, 2020, p. 82

[26] Green, Cliff. "Tomorrow Never Comes". *Order Over Chaos*, 2024, pp 36 - 37

Secret Societies

In today's world, I realize that uniting Black people will be difficult. I don't mean to say it's impossible, but I've seen many of our sisters and brothers dedicate themselves to other causes—causes that take precedence over their identity.

I know a story about a Black man who used to be a cop. As the story goes, whenever he pulled over a Black man, if that man called him "brother," he would say, "I'm not your brother."

I am not suggesting that, simply because we share the same skin color, I should ignore any offense I may have committed or not. But why would a Black man's heart be so cold toward another Black man? Is it solely because he has sworn to be blue instead of Black?

I've had incidents with Black cops that make you question their morals. I remember walking down the street in Southeast when I approached an unmarked burgundy Chevy Impala. There were a bunch of cops surrounding this young man; they had him sitting on the hood of the car.

As I passed them by, I heard one of them say, "Young man." So I turned around to see what the noise was about. One of the cops was walking toward me. He asked me for my ID, and I asked him why. I can hear some White people now, saying, "Just give him your ID." This could be a random man in a costume. I don't know him.

He told me it's a hoodie thing and that someone was just robbed. Like, huh? It was 10 degrees outside, so of course, I was wearing a hoodie. I gave him a stupid face, but I obliged and showed him my ID.

As I'm showing him my ID, a Black cop comes over and asks irrelevant questions. "Where are you from?" Then another Black cop steps up and asks me if I have any weapons on me.

He finally asks if I mind being patted down. I tell him I do. Then the Black cop tries to be the enforcer. The White cop is the one who says there's no need to pat me down. But the Black cop was persistent.

I finally gave in and let him pat me down. But that situation made me question whether a lot of these cops are sweet. I don't want to, nor have I ever wanted to, rub a man's legs and crotch.

I told them, "I appreciated them doing their job and protecting me, but I am not your guy!" I look at the Black cops with disgust and say, 'Pardon my back,' then continued walking to the library.

What seemed to be Black men were enforcing a system's policies on people who might share their DNA. Their pledge to be blue overrides their birthright of being Black.

The same applies to Black fraternities, sororities, and secret societies. Believe me, I understand that not everyone is meant to be part of the group until they prove themselves worthy. That makes complete sense. But how can you call me your brother if you can't share your whole truth?

Fraternities and sororities are another way to divide us. They are like legal gangs. You get initiated into a gang, hazed into a fraternity. You do tough things you might not agree with for a gang, and you do stuff you might not agree with for a fraternity. If you're in one, do you agree with the hazing process?

I understand the history of them starting because we weren't allowed to join White fraternities and sororities. But why did we choose to go Greek rather than Egyptian?

I could be misunderstanding it. From my perspective, I am here to bring clarity. Everything kept in darkness will eventually be revealed in the light. If you ask me a question, I will tell you the truth.

People who know me know I never do or say anything malicious. I act with love. That's why I continually work on improving myself and others. That is why I am not writing this to cause more division. I have friends in fraternities and sororities. Though it isn't my cup of tea, I still love them.

Please enlighten me! Is a group or club stopping you from being honest?

WHO's Ignorant

I'm working to develop more empathy and compassion for people WHO don't know any better. It took me some time to understand that people don't know what they don't know. Because honestly, WHO would expect their elected officials to harm them?

Most people don't realize that the chemicals in their water and food are damaging their health. Unknowingly, they have spent their entire lives ingesting chemicals.

The fluoride and chlorine in your tap water are calcifying your pineal gland. Some say that our pineal gland is where our spiritual eye resides. Put some water in a cup and smell it. Why does it smell like you're about to drink pool water? WHO approved drinking that?

If magnesium oil can be easily absorbed through our skin, wouldn't chlorine and fluoride be able to do the same? But WHO said it was safe to shower in that.

We've all been lied to for a while, so people don't know WHO to trust. I'm here to share what I know and hopefully help you become the healthiest version of yourself.

You should:
- Detox regularly.
- Purchase a water distiller or a reverse osmosis system.
- Install a filter on your shower.
- Use all-natural products on your skin.

- Check the ingredient list on your food. If you don't understand the ingredients, your body won't either.

Honestly, we live in an age where everything has been exposed. Stop trusting your elected officials and anyone claiming authority. They don't have your best interests at heart, because WHO clearly doesn't care.

Recycle 9

We give ourselves every opportunity in the world to avoid doing what we're supposed to do.

I remember using my brother Wolf's Netflix account when you could download anything you wanted. I thought about downloading a show or movie to watch while at work.

First, I shouldn't be watching anything while at work. I should be focused on the task at hand. Second, why am I not using my time at work to further my personal goals? Instead of watching something I didn't create, I should be working on my next book.

I was choosing to distract myself instead of making progress. It's not like I had an excuse not to write. I have the tools I need. But honestly, I was avoiding it out of fear.

Fear is one of the biggest obstacles we all face. Sometimes, when we think about what it takes to achieve something, we feel that fear creeping in. How many times have you talked yourself out of starting something because you were afraid of what the outcome might be?

Remember what I said in Father Time: the longer you procrastinate, the sooner you'll face God. Honestly, that's a scary thought. I don't know about you, but I believe in the Most High God.

Have you ever given someone a gift, only to find out they wasted it? You were probably a little angry. I may have even irritated or pissed you off. You probably said to yourself, "That MotherF'er wasted a gift that I took the time and effort to get them! They got me F'd up!"

What if the same were true in the afterlife? What if you sat before God and twelve angels, and they began asking you questions?

God – "I gave you the ability to sing; why didn't you use the gift I gave you? I gave you so many gifts, and you didn't even unwrap them. You still have some gifts boxed up and stored away. Some gifts you played around with but never took the time to see through. Why?"

How would you answer? It's God and the Twelve; you can't outwit, outsmart, or lie to them. You have to answer honestly, and the answers you give will determine your fate.

Let's set God aside for a moment, because a lot of people don't believe in a higher power. If you asked yourself the same questions, would you be happy with your answers? Are you giving your all to become the best version of yourself?

My brother Justin shared a motto that I love: "Die empty!" This means to give your all in this life. Don't leave behind untouched gifts and abilities.

Don't let fear block you from reaching your potential. You didn't get the girl you liked because you were afraid of rejection. You didn't start the business because you were scared it might fail. You can't let fear hold you back. The list goes on and on. Everything you didn't achieve but had the power to do was probably because of fear. But you will never know until you try.

I know we sometimes fear intangible things, like what others think of us. What will my family and friends think? Look, forget all that. Forget about what anybody else might think of you.

Don't be on your deathbed saying, "I wish I had..." The moment those words come out of your mouth, you'll be facing God, and He'll say, "You wish you would've what?"

Will you keep letting fear hold you back? I hope not, because what if waste made you recycle 9?

I Salute You!

I sincerely thank you for sticking with me this far. This is the third book in the **A tREAL O.G.** series, and it took years to create. I poured my heart, soul, and mind into it, and I hope the emotions come through on the pages.

This book was created to support people with similar experiences and offers insights for those interested in understanding the mindset of a tREAL Black man.

My goal is to reach the world, especially the youth, before the world attempts to corrupt them. So, if these stories have resonated with you, please leave a review. Every review helps this book reach more people.

I'd love to connect and build with you. If you're interested in doing the same, please follow me at @cliffgr33n. For updates on upcoming projects and merchandise, visit www.cliffgr33n.com.

tREAL 1111111111111111111111111111111 salute!

Thank you again for tuning in. May you and your loved ones enjoy abundant Peace, Power, and Prosperity!

<u>A tREAL O.G. > A Trill O.G. > A Trilogy</u>

Less Than a Sack of Weed ©
Order Over Chaos ©
÷ 9 ©